HUMBLE THYSELF
BEFORE THE LORD

Humble Thyself
before the Lord

THOMAS À KEMPIS
BROTHER LAWRENCE
ST. ANTONY OF EGYPT
ST. CATHERINE OF SIENA

PARACLETE PRESS
BREWSTER, MASSACHUSETTS

2014 First printing

Humble Thyself Before the Lord

ISBN 978-1-61261-503-5

Consists of excerpts from material previously published by Paraclete Press, Inc.

Library of Congress Cataloging-in-Publication Data is available.

10 9 8 7 6 5 4 3 2 1

Published by Paraclete Press
Brewster, Massachusetts
www.paracletepress.com

Printed in the United States of America

CONTENTS

FOREWORD

It is not easy to write about the importance of Christian humility. How does one exhort others to be humble without sounding boastful oneself? The writings in this volume avoid that problem. They are classics of the genre of Christian spiritual writing, penned by four of the true experts on the Christian spiritual life.

Each of them writes with clarity, and from a great depth of personal experience, and yet what they describe is something that is ultimately beyond description. In that respect, this book is deceptively simple: you cannot obtain what they describe by simply reading.

The writings are not presented chronologically, but rather, thematically, in a way that is designed to move the reader from one topic to the next in an order of spiritual progression.

Brief biographies of each author may be found at the conclusion of the book.

THOMAS À KEMPIS

From *The Imitation of Christ*

HUMILITY IS THE GREATEST WISDOM

From *The Imitation of Christ*, book I, 1–2

CHAPTER 1

The Imitation, or Following of Christ, and Contempt for All the Vanities of the World

1. "Whoever follows me," says the Lord, "will not walk in darkness but will have the light of life."[1] These are the words of Christ, by which we are taught to follow his life and way of life if we would be truly enlightened and delivered from all blindness of heart. Let it therefore be our chief endeavor to meditate upon the life of Jesus Christ.

2. The teaching of Jesus Christ excels all the teachings of the saints. One who has the Spirit, will find in it the hidden manna.[2]

But it happens that many, although they often hear the Gospel of Christ, are moved by it very little, because they do not have the Spirit of Christ.

Therefore, those who would fully and wholeheartedly understand the words of Christ, must endeavor to conform their lives entirely to the life of Christ.

3. What will you gain if you dispute learnedly on the doctrine of the Trinity, if you lack humility, and by this you are displeasing to the Trinity?

Surely great words do not make us holy and righteous; but a virtuous life makes us dear to God.[3]

I would rather feel contrition than know its definition.

If you knew the whole Bible by heart, and the sayings of all the philosophers, what would this profit you without the love and grace of God?

"Vanity of vanities! All is vanity"—except to love God and to serve him alone.[4] This is the highest wisdom: to despise the world and to look for the kingdom of heaven.[5]

4. It is therefore vanity to look for the perishing riches, and to trust in them.[6]

It is also vanity to look for honors and to attempt to climb to a high position.

It is vanity to follow the desires of the flesh and yearn for that which must bring with it grievous punishment.

It is vanity to desire to live long and not to care to live well.

It is vanity to be concerned only with this present life, and to make no provision for the life that is to come.

It is vanity to love that which so speedily perishes and decays, and not to hurry on to where everlasting joy awaits you.

5. Call often to mind that proverb, "The eye is not satisfied with seeing, or the ear filled with hearing."[7]

Endeavor then, to withdraw your heart from the love of things that are seen, and to turn yourself to the things that are unseen.[8]

For those who follow their own sensual lusts defile their consciences and lose the grace of God.[9]

CHAPTER 2
Thinking Humbly of Ourselves

1. All persons naturally desire knowledge;[10] but what good is knowledge without the fear of God?

Surely a humble peasant who serves God is better than a proud philosopher who, neglecting his own soul, occupies himself in studying the course of the stars.

Those who truly know themselves are lowly in their own eyes, and do not delight in the praises of others.

If I understood everything in the world and did not have divine love, what would it avail me in the sight of God, who will judge me according to my deeds?[11]

2. Give up that excessive desire for knowledge, for in it there is much distraction and deception.

Learned persons are anxious to appear learned to others, and to be called wise.

There are many things the knowledge of which does little or no good to the soul.

And they are very unwise who set their minds on anything more than they do on the things that aid them in their salvation.

Many words do not satisfy the soul, but a good life comforts the heart, and a clean conscience gives great confidence toward God.[12]

3. The more you know and the better you understand, the more strictly you will be judged, unless your life is also more holy.

Do not be elated in your own mind, then, because of any ability or knowledge you may possess, but rather let the knowledge given you make you more humble and cautious.

If you think that you understand and know much, know also that there are many more things you do not know.

So do not be proud and puffed up with your knowledge,[13] but rather acknowledge your own ignorance.[14] Why would you set yourself above others, since there are many more learned and more skillful in the Scripture than you are?

If you would know or learn anything to your own good, then desire to be unknown and to be considered as nothing.[15]

4. The highest and most profitable learning is a true knowledge and humble opinion of oneself.

It is great wisdom and perfection to think nothing of ourselves, and always to think well and highly of others.

If you should see another openly sin or commit some grievous offense, you should still not think yourself better because of it; for you do not know how long you will be able to stand.

We are all weak and frail; but you should regard no one frailer than yourself.

CULTIVATING A HUMBLE SPIRIT

From *The Imitation of Christ,* book I, 6–11

CHAPTER 6
Inordinate Affections

1. Whenever we desire anything inordinately,[16] we are at once disquieted within ourselves.

The proud and covetous can never rest. The poor and humble in spirit dwell in the multitude of peace.

Those who are not completely dead to themselves are quickly tempted and overcome in small and trifling things.

The weak in spirit, and those who are as yet in bondage to fleshly and material things, can withdraw themselves from worldly desires only with great difficulty.

Therefore, they are often afflicted and sad when they set about to withdraw themselves from those desires and are quickly angered when any opposition comes against them.

2. If they have given in to their lusts and obtained what they desired, they are soon plagued with remorse of conscience, because they yielded to their passion and in this way robbed themselves of the very peace they sought.

True quietness of heart, therefore, is achieved by resisting our passions, not by obeying them.

There is no peace in the heart of a fleshly person, nor of one who is wholly given up to outward things; but in a fervent, spiritual person who takes delight in God there is found great peace and inward quietness.

CHAPTER 7
Avoiding Vain Hope and Pride

1. They are foolish indeed who put their trust in other persons or in any creature.

Do not be ashamed to serve others for the love of Jesus Christ and to be considered poor in this world.

Do not presume to trust yourself, but place your hope in God.[17]

Do what is in your power to do, and God will honor your heart's intent.

Do not trust in your own knowledge,[18] or in the cleverness of any living soul, but rather in the grace of God, who helps the humble and humbles the proud.[19]

2. If you have wealth, do not glory in it or in your powerful friends. Rather glory in God who gives all things and who, above all, desires to give you himself.

Do not pride yourself because of your physical stature or your beauty, which may be marred or destroyed by a small illness.

Do not take pleasure in your natural gifts or your readiness of wit, for fear that you may offend God, who created everything good that you have received by nature.

3. Do not consider yourself better than others, for fear that perhaps in the sight of God, who knows what is in us, you be accounted worse than they are.

Do not be proud in well-doing, for the judgment of God is far different from human judgment, and he is often offended by that which we find pleasing.

If there is any good in you, you should believe that there is much more in others, and so preserve your humility.

It does you no harm to consider yourself worse than all other persons, but it does you great harm to exalt yourself above even one person.

The humble enjoy continual peace, but the heart of the proud is full of jealousy and frequent indignation.

CHAPTER 8
Avoiding Too Much Familiarity

1. Do not lay open your heart to everyone, but in all your affairs, go in search of the counsel of those who are wise and who fear God.

Do not talk much with the young nor with strangers.

Do not flatter the rich, or go in search of the presence of great and famous persons.

Keep company with the simple and humble, with the devout and upright. Talk with them about uplifting things. Do not be familiar with any woman, but in general commend all good women to God.

Desire to have close fellowship with God alone and with his holy angels, and avoid the acquaintance of other persons as much as you may.

2. We must have charity toward everyone, but familiarity with everyone is not advisable.

Sometimes it happens that a person unknown to us is highly commended by the good reports of others, but turns out to be offensive on closer contact.

We think sometimes that we please others by our presence when in fact we are offensive to them by those bad qualities that they can see in us.

CHAPTER 9
Obedience and Subjection

1. It is a very great thing to live in obedience, to be under a superior, and not to be free to do as we please.

It is much safer to obey than to govern.

Many live under obedience more from necessity than from love, and such persons are discontented and easily complain. They cannot attain freedom of mind unless they willingly and heartily put themselves under obedience for the love of God.

Go wherever you will, but you will still find no rest except in humble subjection under the government of a superior. Many have deceived themselves, imagining they would find happiness in change.

2. It is true that all of us readily do the thing that most agrees with our own liking, and are most drawn to those who are like-minded.

But if God is among us, we must sometimes for the sake of peace let go of our own opinions.

Who is so wise that they can fully know all things?

Do not, therefore, be too confident in your own opinion, but be willing to hear the judgment of others.

If what you think is really sound and yet you give it up for God and follow the opinion of another, it will be turned to your greater good.

3. I have often heard that it is safer to hear and take counsel than to give it.

It may also happen that each one's opinion may be good; but to refuse to yield to others when reason or special cause require it, is a mark of pride and stubbornness.

CHAPTER 10
Avoiding Too Much Talk

1. Avoid the disorderly agitation of the world as much as possible, because talk of worldly affairs is a great hindrance, even though it might be done with good intentions.

For we are quickly deceived and captured by things that have no real value.

I often wish I had held my tongue when I have spoken, and that I had not been in the company of others.

Why do we so eagerly speak and talk with one another when we so seldom return to silence without suffering harm to our conscience?

The reason is that we look for comfort from one another in such talk and want to ease our mind, which is excessively burdened with our many thoughts.

We very eagerly talk and think of those things we most love or desire, or of the things we dislike most.

2. But how grievous this is! It is often in vain and to no good, because the outward satisfaction of our talk caused us great loss of inward and divine consolation.

Therefore we must watch and pray, so that our time will not pass away idly.

If it is permissible and expedient for you to talk, speak of those things that may uplift the other.

Evil habits and neglect of our own growth in grace are the chief causes of our thoughtless and idle talk.

Yet talking of spiritual things greatly aids our spiritual growth, especially when persons of one mind and spirit are gathered together in God.

CHAPTER 11
Attaining Peace and Growth in Grace

1. We would enjoy much peace if we did not occupy ourselves with the words and activities of others, and with things that are of no concern to us.[20]

How can persons remain long in peace who intrude into the affairs of others, who look for occasions to travel about, and who seldom give serious thought to themselves?

Blessed are the single-hearted, for they will enjoy much peace.[21]

2. Why were many of the saints so perfect and contemplative?

Because they labored to die completely to all earthly desires, and therefore they could with their whole heart adhere firmly and closely to God and give themselves wholly to God.

We are led too much by our feelings, and we are too concerned about transitory things.

We seldom overcome even one fault perfectly. We have too little eagerness to grow spiritually every day, and so we remain cold and lukewarm.

3. If we were perfectly dead to ourselves, and not entangled with outward things, we would be able to taste and relish spiritual things, and to have some experience of heavenly contemplation.

The greatest, and indeed the only, hindrance is that we are not free from passions and lusts, and we do not attempt to walk in the perfect way of the saints. When some small difficulty arises, we are quickly cast down in spirits and turn to people for consolation.

4. If we tried like brave persons to stand in this spiritual battle, surely we would experience the help of God from heaven.

The One who gives us the occasion to fight to the end so that we may obtain the victory is ready to help those who fight, trusting in his grace.[22]

If we rely only on some outward observances for progress in our spiritual life, our devotion will quickly run out.

But let us lay the axe to the root, so that being freed from our passions, we may find rest for our souls.

5. If we would root out one fault every year, we would soon become mature.

But as it is now, we often notice, on the contrary, that we were better and purer at the beginning of our conversion than after many years of our profession.

Our fervor and our progress should increase daily; but it is now considered a great thing if we can retain even some part of our initial zeal.

If we would do even a little violence against ourselves at the beginning, we would be able to perform everything with ease and delight.

6. It is a hard matter to give up evil habits, but it is even harder to go against our own will.

If you cannot overcome the small and easy things, how will you overcome the harder ones?

Resist your evil inclinations at the very start, and break evil habits, for fear that they will pull you little by little into even greater trouble.

If you only knew how much inward peace to yourself and joy to others your good outward manner would obtain, I think you would take more care about your spiritual growth.

ONLY THE HUMBLE CAN HEAR GOD'S WORD

From *The Imitation of Christ*, book III, 3–4

CHAPTER 3

Hearing God's Word with Humility

1. My child, hear my words, words of greatest sweetness, far surpassing the knowledge of the philosophers and the wise of this world.

"The words that I have spoken to you are spirit and life,"[23] and cannot be fully comprehended by human understanding.

They are not to be perverted for vain conceit, but are to be heard in silence and received with great humility and great affection of the heart.

Blessed are those, Lord, whom you instruct and teach out of your law, giving them rest in the evil days, and not leaving them desolate on this earth.[24]

2. I taught the prophets from the beginning (says the Lord), yet I do not cease to speak to every creature even to this day; but many are hardened and are deaf to my voice.

Most people listen more gladly to the world than to God; they would rather follow the desires of the flesh than the good pleasure of God.

The world promises temporal things of small value, and yet it is served with great eagerness. I promise things that are most high and eternal, and yet human hearts remain slow and dull.

Who is there who serves and obeys me in all things with such care as people serve and obey the world and its rulers? "Be ashamed, O Sidon," says the sea![25] And do you ask why this is?

People undertake a long journey for a little reward; for eternal life many will hardly lift one foot from the ground.

They seek after the most pitiful reward; for a single penny sometimes there is shameful contention. For a slight promise or a little trifle people do not hesitate to toil day and night.

3. But, what a deep pity this is! For an unchangeable good, for a reward beyond all price, for the highest honor, for glory that has no end, they begrudge the slightest fatigue.

Be ashamed, then, slothful and complaining servant, that they are more ready for the labor of death than you are for the labor of life.

They rejoice more in seeking vanity than you do in seeking the truth.

They are often disappointed in that in which they hope, but my promise deceives no one, and sends no one empty away who trusts in me.[26]

What I have promised, I will give, and what I have said, I will fulfill, if only a person will remain faithful in my love even to the end.

I am the rewarder of all good persons[27] and the strong approver of all the devout.[28]

A Prayer for the Grace of Devotion

5. Lord my God! you are my entire good. And who am I that I presume to speak to you? I am the poorest and most worthless of your servants, a wretched worm, much poorer and more contemptible than I know or dare express.

Yet remember, Lord, that I am nothing, I have nothing, and can do nothing.

You alone are good, just, and holy; you can do all things, you give all things, leaving only the sinner empty.

Remember your mercies, and fill my heart with your grace, for you do not will that your works should be in vain.

6. How can I bear the miseries of this life unless you give me strength by your mercy and grace in it?

Do not turn your face away from me.[29]

Do not delay your visitation, or withdraw your consolation, or my soul will become a dry, thirsty land.

Teach me, Lord, to do your will.[30] Teach me to walk worthily and humbly before you. For you are my wisdom; you know me in truth, and knew me before the world was made and long before I was born into the world.

CHAPTER 4
Walking Before God in Truth and Humility

1. My child, walk before me in truth and always seek me in the singleness of your heart.[31] Those who walk before me in truth will be safe from the assaults of evil and the truth will set them free[32] from seducers and from the malice of the wicked.

"If the truth makes you free, you will be free indeed," and you will not care for the vain words of persons.

Lord, it is true! As you say, so let it be with me, I pray. Let the truth teach me, guard me, and preserve me to the end.

Let it set me free from all evil affection and from all inordinate love, and I will walk with you in great liberty of heart.

2. I will teach you (says the Truth) what is acceptable and pleasing in my sight.

Reflect on your sins with great displeasure and sorrow of heart, and never consider yourself to be anything because of your good works.

In truth you are a sinner—you are subject to and entangled with many passions. Of yourself you always tend to nothingness. You soon fall, are quickly overcome, quickly disturbed, quickly unnerved.

You have nothing in which to glory[33] but many things for which you should consider yourself abhorrent, for you are much weaker than you are able to comprehend.

3. Let nothing you do, then, seem great, nothing precious or wonderful, nothing worthy of esteem, nothing high, nothing truly commendable or desirable except what is eternal.

Let the eternal truth please you above all things; let your own utter contemptibleness always displease you.

Fear nothing so much, blame nothing so much as your own vices and sins, which ought to be more displeasing to you than any loss whatsoever of goods.

Some do not walk before me in sincerity, but being led by curiosity and pride, they desire to know my secret things and to understand the deep things of God, while they neglect themselves and their salvation.

These often fall into great temptations and sins through their pride and curiosity when I resist them.

Fear the judgments of God. Tremble before the wrath of the Almighty. Shrink from searching out the works of the Most High, but search narrowly into your own wickedness, into how many ways you have offended, and how much good you have neglected.

There are some who carry their devotion only in books, some in pictures, some in outward signs and figures.

Some have me on their lips, but little in their heart.

There are others who, enlightened in their understanding and purified in their affection, always long after eternal things, hear of earthly things with reluctance, and obey the necessities of nature with sorrow. And these feel what the Spirit of Truth speaks in them.

For the Spirit teaches them to despise the things of the earth, to love heavenly things, to disregard the world, and to desire heaven all day and night.

FOUR THINGS THAT BRING PEACE

From *The Imitation of Christ*, book III, 23–27

CHAPTER 23

Four Things that Bring Peace

1. Child, I will teach you the way of peace and true freedom.

2. Lord, I pray, do as you say, for this is delightful for me to hear.

3. Child, make this your aim, to do the will of another rather than your own.[34]

Always choose to have less rather than more.[35]

Always seek the lower place, to be under the authority of all.[36]

Always desire and pray that the will of God may be wholly fulfilled in you.[37]

Anyone who does this enters within the borders of peace and rest.

4. Lord, this short discourse of yours contains much perfection.[38]

It is few in words, but full in meaning and abundant in fruit.

If I could faithfully keep it, I would not be so easily troubled.

For as often as I feel myself disturbed and discontent, I find that I have strayed from this teaching.

But you can do all things and always desire the progress of my soul. Increase your grace in me, so that I may be able to fulfill your words and perfect my salvation.

A Prayer Against Evil Thoughts

5. O God, do not be far from me. O my God, make haste to help me![39] For vain thoughts have risen up against me, and great fears have troubled my soul.

How will I pass through them unhurt? How will I break them down?

6. I will go before you, says the Lord, and humble the great ones of the earth. Then I will open the prison doors and show you hidden things in secret places.[40]

7. Lord, do as you say, and let all evil thoughts flee from before your face.

Truly this is my hope and my one consolation, to flee to you in every trouble, to trust in you, inwardly to call on you, and patiently to await your consolation.

A Prayer for Mental Illumination

8. Enlighten me, good Jesus, with the brightness of your inward light, and take away all darkness from my heart.

Take away the multitude of my wandering thoughts, and crush those temptations that so violently assail me.

Fight mightily for me and drive away those evil beasts, those enticing lusts of the flesh, and in this way speak peace through your strength. Then the abundance of your praise may sound in the holy court that is a pure conscience.

Command the winds and storms. Say to the sea, "Be still," and to the north wind, "Do not blow!" and there will be a great calm.

9. Send out your light and your truth that they may shine on the earth,[41] for until you enlighten me, I am as earth that is empty and void.

Pour forth your grace from above and water my heart with the dew of heaven; send down the waters of devotion to wash the face of the earth, so that it may bring forth good and perfect fruit.

Lift up my mind, oppressed as it is with the load of sins, and raise my whole desire toward heavenly things, so that having tasted the sweetness of things above, I may find it irksome even to think of things below.

10. Take me, and snatch me away from all the fleeting consolations of created things; for no created thing can fully fill and satisfy my longing. Join me to yourself with the inseparable bonds of love, for you alone are sufficient for one who loves you, and without you the whole universe is only frivolity.

CHAPTER 24
Inordinate Curiosity

1. Child, do not be curious nor trouble yourself with those things that do not belong to you.

What is this thing or that to you? Follow me.[42]

What is it to you whether this person is good or bad, or whether that person says or does this or that?

You will not need to answer for others, but you must give account of yourself. Why, then, do you entangle yourself?

Look, I know everyone, and see everything that is done under the sun, and I understand how it is with everyone: what they think, what they want, and what their intentions are.

Therefore, all these concerns are to be committed to me; but, as for you, keep yourself in peace, and let busybodies be as busy as they will.

Whatever they will do or say will come upon themselves, for they cannot deceive me.

2. Do not seek the shadow of a great name, or the familiar friendship of many, or the particular and exclusive affection of anyone.

For these things produce much distraction of mind and will bring great darkness into your soul.

I would gladly speak my word and reveal my secrets to you if you would diligently watch for my coming and open to me the door of your heart.

Be circumspect and watchful in prayer, and humble yourself in all things.[43]

CHAPTER 25
Peace of Heart and True Spiritual Progress

1. Child, I have said, peace I leave with you; my peace I give to you. I do not give to you as the world gives.[44] Everyone desires peace, but not everyone cares for the things that make for true peace.

My peace is with the humble and gentle of heart. Your peace will be in much patience.

If you will hear me and follow my words, you will enjoy much peace.

—What then will I do?

In everything take heed to yourself, what you are doing and what you are saying, and direct your whole attention to please me alone, not desiring or seeking anything apart from me.

As for the words or deeds of others, do not judge anything rashly, or busy yourself with things not committed to your care. If you do this, it may be that you are seldom or little disturbed.

2. But never to feel any disturbance at all, or to suffer any grief of heart or body, does not belong to this present life but to the state of eternal rest.

Do not think, then, that you have found true peace if you feel no heaviness, or that all is well when you have no adversity, or that all is perfect if all things happen as you desire.

Do not think at all highly of yourself, or account yourself to be especially beloved if you are in a state of great devotion and sweetness, for it is not in such things that a true lover of virtue is known, nor does the true progress and perfection of a person consist in these things.

—In what then, Lord?

In giving yourself with all your heart to the divine will; in not seeking your own interest in either great matters or small, in time or in eternity.

In this way you will be able with the same equal demeanor to give thanks both in prosperity and adversity, weighing all things in an equal balance.

If you should come to be so valiant and patient in hope that when inward consolation is withdrawn, you can prepare your heart to suffer even more, and yet do not justify yourself as though you should not suffer such great afflictions, but acknowledge my justice in all my appointments, and do not cease to praise my holy name:

Then you are walking in the true and right way of peace, and you may hope without any doubt to see my face again with great joy.

If you arrive at an utter contempt of yourself, know that you will then enjoy an abundance of peace as great as is possible in the state of your temporary stay here.

CHAPTER 26
Gaining Freedom of Mind Through Humility

1. Lord, this is the work of persons who desire to be perfect, never to let their minds slacken from attention to heavenly things and to pass through the many cares as if they had no care—not in sluggish passivity, but with the certainty of a

free mind that does not cling to any created thing or person with inordinate affection.

2. I earnestly beg of you, most compassionate God, to preserve me from the cares of this life, so that I not become too entangled in them; preserve me from the many necessities of the body, so that I may not be ensnared by pleasures of the flesh. And preserve me from all hindrances of the soul, for fear that, being disheartened, I should be cast down.

I do not speak only of such vanities as worldly persons covet with eager desire, but of the miseries that are the common lot of humankind, miseries that grieve the souls of your servants and keep them back and make them unable to enter into the freedom of the Spirit whenever they desire.

3. My God, unspeakable sweetness, make bitter to me all fleshly delights that would draw me away from the love of eternal things, and would wickedly entice me to sin by setting before me some present delight.

Do not let flesh and blood prevail against me, my God, do not let them prevail! Do not let the world and its brief glory deceive me! Do not let the devil and his devices trip me up!

Give me strength to resist, patience to endure, and constancy to persevere.

Give me, instead of all the consolations of this world, the sweetest anointing of your Spirit, and instead of fleshly love, send into my soul the love of your name.

4. See, food, drink, clothing, and other necessities of the body are burdensome to a fervent spirit.

Grant me to use such refreshments with moderation, and not to be entangled with an excessive desire for them.

It is not allowed us to cast them all away, for nature must be sustained. But your holy law forbids us to seek an excess of things for mere pleasure; for then the flesh would grow contemptuous against the spirit. Between these, let your hand govern and direct me, I earnestly ask you, so that nothing will be done in excess.

CHAPTER 27
The Evil of Self-Love

1. Child, it behooves you to give all for all, and to keep nothing of yourself from me.

Know that self-love hurts you more than anything else in the world.

Things cling to you and hold you to a greater or lesser degree, according to the love you have for them.

If your love is pure, simple, and well ordered, you will be free from bondage to any earthly thing.[45]

Do not sinfully desire anything that is not lawful for you to have, and do not seek to have anything that may hinder you or deprive you of inward liberty.

It is strange that you do not commit yourself fully to me with all your heart, together with everything you may have or desire.

2. Why do you consume yourself with vain grief?[46] Why do you weary yourself with needless cares?

Submit to my good pleasure and you will not suffer any loss.

If you seek this or that, and want to be in this place or that, to enjoy your own advantage and good pleasure, you will never be at rest or free from anxiety, for in everything you will find some defect and in every place there will be someone to cross you.

3. It is not, then, obtaining or multiplying outward things that serves to your advantage, but rather despising and rooting them out of your heart.

This is not to be understood only of money and riches, but also with regard to the quest for honor and the desire for vain praise, which quickly vanish and pass away with the world.

No place suffices if the spirit of fervor is lacking. Any peace that comes from outward things cannot stand long if the true foundation of the heart is lacking. You may change your place, then, but not make yourself any better.

For when the new occasions arise, you will find in them the same thing from which you fled—yes, and even more!

Prayer for a Pure Heart and for Wisdom

4. Strengthen me, God, by the grace of the Holy Spirit.[47]

Give me grace to be strong in the inner self[48] and to cast out of my heart all needless care and anxiety,[49] so that I will not be drawn away by vacillating desires for anything whatever, whether it be of great value or little; but teach me to look on all things as passing away and myself as soon to pass away with them.

For nothing is lasting under the sun, where all is vanity and vexation of spirit. How wise are those who consider it to be so.

5. Give me, Lord, heavenly wisdom[50] so that I may learn to seek and find you above all things, to relish and love you above all things, and to understand all other things as they really are, as ordained in your wisdom.

Give me grace wisely to avoid those who flatter me, and to bear patiently with those who oppose me; for it is great wisdom not to be blown about by every wind of words,[51] or to give ear to the false flattery of the siren. In this way I will go on securely in the way I have begun.

BROTHER LAWRENCE

From *The Practice of the Presence of God*

PRACTICING HUMILITY IN GOD'S PRESENCE

From *The Practice of the Presence of God*, part IV

The Spiritual Maxims

All things are possible to one who believes, even more to one who hopes, and still more to one who loves; but all things are even more possible to one who practices these three virtues and perseveres in them. All who are baptized believers have made the first step on the road that leads to perfection, and will be perfect providing they persevere in the practice of the following guides to their conduct:

First. We must always keep our eyes on God and His glory in all we do, say, or undertake. May the goal toward which we strive be to become perfect worshipers of God in this life, just as we hope to be throughout all eternity. Resolve firmly to overcome, by the grace of God, all the difficulties found in the spiritual life.

Second. When we undertake the spiritual life, we must consider in depth who we are, and we will find ourselves worthy of all scorn, unworthy of the name of Christian, and subject to all sorts of afflictions and countless misfortunes. We will find that these woes not only trouble us but also make us uncertain in our health, in our moods, and in our inner and outward dispositions. In short, we will find ourselves among those whom God chooses to make humble through an abundance of sufferings and travails, both within and without.

Third. We must believe beyond any doubt that it is to our advantage to sacrifice ourselves to God and that He is pleased by our sacrifice. It is normal in His divine Providence that we should be abandoned to all sorts of conditions, sufferings, afflictions, and temptations for the love of God, as much and for as long as it is His will. Without this submission of heart and spirit to the will of God, there can be no devotion or going on to perfection.

Fourth. A soul is all the more dependent on grace as it aspires to higher perfection, and the help and assistance of God are all the more necessary to us every moment because without Him the soul can do nothing. The world, the flesh, and the devil all combine to make such a strong and continual war against the soul that without the very present help of God and our humble and necessary dependence upon Him, they would carry it away in spite of itself. To our nature this seems harsh, but grace takes pleasure in being dependent upon God and finds its rest in Him.

ONE
Practices Necessary to Acquire the Spiritual Life

First. The holiest, most universal and most necessary practice in the spiritual life is the presence of God. To practice the presence of God is to take pleasure in and become accustomed to His Divine company, speaking humbly and conversing lovingly in our hearts with Him at all times and at every moment, especially in times of temptation, pain, spiritual dryness, revulsion to spiritual things, and even unfaithfulness and sin.

Second. We must apply ourselves continually to the end that all our actions may be little spontaneous conversations with God, coming from purity and simplicity of heart.

Third. We must weigh all our actions without the impetuosity or impulsiveness that mark a distraught spirit. As we carry out our duties, we must work gently, tranquilly, and lovingly with God, asking Him to accept our labor. Through our continual attention to God, we will crush the head of the devil and make his weapons fall from his hands.

Fourth. During our work and other activities, and even during our times of reading or writing, even though they may be spiritually oriented—and yes, even more during our outward devotions and prayers aloud—we ought to stop for a short moment, as frequently as we can, to adore God deep within our hearts and take pleasure in Him, even though we might have to do this momentarily and in secret. Since you are not unmindful of the fact that God is present before you as you carry out your duties, and you know that He is at the depth and center of your soul, why not stop from time to time, whatever you are doing—even if you are praying aloud—to adore Him inwardly, to praise Him, to beseech Him, to offer your heart to Him, and to thank Him?

What could please God more than for us to leave all created things over and over each day in this way in order to withdraw and worship Him in our hearts? Not to mention the fact that this is the way to destroy self-love, which cannot exist except among us creatures. Inwardly returning to God in this way rids us of self-love without our even being aware of it.

Finally, we can give no greater witness to God of our faithfulness than by continually renouncing and turning from the created things around us to take pleasure, even for a single moment, in our Creator.

This is not to suggest that you should withdraw inwardly forever. That is not possible. But prudence, the mother of virtues, will guide you. Nonetheless, I maintain that it is a common error among spiritual persons not to withdraw from outward things from time to time to worship God within themselves and to find comfort and pleasure in the peace of His Divine presence for a few moments.

This digression has been lengthy, but I thought that the matter demanded all this explanation. Let us return to our discussion of spiritual practices.

Fifth. All this adoration must be done in faith, believing that in truth God is in our hearts, that we must worship, love, and serve

Him in spirit and truth, and that He sees all that is happening or will happen in us and in all creatures. We must believe that He is altogether independent of everything and that He is the One on whom every created thing depends. He is infinitely perfect and is worthy by His infinite excellence and His sovereignty of all that we are and of all that is in heaven and on earth. We must believe that He can dispose according to His good pleasure in time and in eternity, and that we justly owe Him all our thoughts, our words, and our actions. Let us see that we do it!

Sixth. We must study carefully which virtues we need most, those which are the most difficult to acquire, the sins into which we often fall, and the most frequent and inevitable occasions of our falls. We must run back to God with complete confidence when an occasion for spiritual warfare arises, remaining steadfast in the presence of His Divine majesty, humbly worshiping Him and presenting our miseries and afflictions to Him, and asking Him lovingly for the help of His grace. By doing this, in God we will discover all virtues without having any ourselves.

TWO
How to Worship God in Spirit and Truth

There are three answers to this question.

First. To worship God in spirit and truth means to worship God as we ought to worship Him. God is Spirit, so we must worship Him in spirit and truth; that is, with a humble and true spiritual adoration in the depth and center of our souls that God alone can see. We can repeat it so often that in the end it will become a part of our very natures and will be as if God were one with our souls, and our souls one with Him.

Second. To worship God in truth is to recognize Him for who He is, and to recognize ourselves for what we are. To worship God in truth is to recognize as a very present reality in our spirit that God is infinitely perfect, infinitely worthy of worship, and infinitely distanced from evil. He is infinitely greater than all the divine attributes ascribed to Him by man. What man, lacking in wisdom though he may be, could refuse to employ all his strength to respect and worship this great and infinitely worthy God?

Third. To worship God in truth is further to admit that we are entirely contrary to Him, but that He is willing to make us like Himself if we desire it. What man could be so imprudent as to turn himself away, even for a moment, from the reverence, love, service, and continual adoration that we most justly owe Him?

THREE
On the Union of the Soul with God

There are three kinds of spiritual union: the first is habitual, the second is virtual, and the third is actual, that is, accomplished in the present.

First. Habitual union is when we are united to God solely by grace.

Second. Virtual union is when we have begun to unite ourselves to God and we remain united with Him as long as we continue our efforts.

Third. Actual union—present, sustained, ongoing union—is the most perfect of the three. As it is wholly spiritual, its action can be felt within the soul because the soul is not asleep, as it is in the case of the other two unions. On the contrary, it finds itself powerfully excited. Its actions are livelier than those of a fire, more luminous than a sun unobscured by clouds.

We must be careful not to be deceived into thinking that this union is a simple expression of the heart, as in saying, "My God, I love You with all my heart," or other similar words. No, this union is something indefinable that is found in a gentle, peaceable, spiritual, reverent, humble, loving, and utterly simple soul. This "indefinable something" raises the soul and presses it to love God, to worship Him, and yes, even to caress Him with an inexpressible tenderness known only to those who experience it.

Fourth. All who aspire to union with God should know that everything that can delight the will and is pleasant and delicious to it serves to further this union.

We must all acknowledge that it is impossible for our human minds to understand God. In order to unite ourselves to Him, we must deprive our wills of every kind of spiritual and bodily pleasure, so that being thus freed, we can love God *in our wills* above all things. For if the will can in some way understand God, it can only be through love. There is a great deal of difference between the feelings of the will and the operation of the will, since the *feelings* of the will come to an end in the soul, whereas the *operation* of the will, which is the expression of true love, ends up at God.

FOUR
On Practicing the Presence of God

First. Practicing the presence of God is the application of our spirit to God; it is the vivid recollection that God is present with us. It can be accomplished either through the imagination or by the understanding.

Second. I know a person who for forty years has practiced the conscious presence of God. To this practice he gives several other names: sometimes he calls it a simple action, a clear and distinct knowledge of God. Sometimes he refers to it as a blurred, indistinct sight, a general and loving gaze at God, or simply the remembrance of God. At other times he calls it attention to God, a silent conversation with God, confidence in God, or the life and peace of the soul. In short, this person has told me that all these types of the presence of God are only different ways of saying the same thing, and that the presence of God is now so natural that it has become a part of him. Here is how it happened:

Third. Through choosing in his will to frequently recall his spirit into the presence of God, the habit of doing this has been formed in him in such a way that as soon as his mind is free from its outward duties, and frequently even when he is the busiest with them, the uppermost part of his spirit or the highest part of his soul lifts itself without any diligence on his part, and remains as if it were suspended and firmly held on God, above and beyond all things, as if it were in its center and its place of rest. It is by faith that he almost always feels himself in this suspension, and that is sufficient for him. This is what he calls the state of being actually present with God, so that he now lives as if there were only God and himself in the world. He converses with God no matter where he goes, asking God for what he needs and unceasing delighting himself in Him in countless ways.

Fourth. However, it is fitting to repeat that this conversation with God is done in the depth and at the center of the soul. It is there that the soul speaks to God, heart to heart, always delighting itself in God in a state of great and profound peace. All that happens outside seems to the soul like only a small fire that is extinguished as quickly as it is lit, with the result that outward things succeed to a very little degree or almost never in troubling its interior peace.

Fifth. To come back to our discussion of the presence of God, I maintain that this gentle and loving gaze upon God lights a divine fire in the soul without our being aware of it, and this fire burns so ardently with the love of God that we find ourselves obliged to do a number of outward things in order to moderate it.

Sixth. We would be quite surprised if we knew what the soul sometimes says to God, who seems to take such great pleasure in these conversations that He permits the soul complete freedom, provided that it wishes to remain always with Him and rely on Him. And, as though He were afraid that the soul might return to created things, God takes care to supply it so well with all that it can desire that over and over it finds deep within itself a source of nourishment that is very savory and delicious to its taste, although it never desired it or procured it in any way, and without its having contributed anything on its part other than its consent.

Seventh. We can conclude that the practice of the presence of God is the life and nourishment of the soul and that it can be obtained with the grace of the Lord. Here are the means of acquiring it:

FIVE

The Means of Acquiring the Presence of God

First. The first means is leading a very pure life.

Second. The second is remaining very faithful to the practice of this presence and to the interior awareness of God in ourselves. We ought always to do this gently, humbly, and lovingly, without allowing ourselves to be troubled or worried.

Third. We must take care to glance inwardly toward God, even for a moment, before proceeding with our outward actions. Then, as we go about our duties, we must continue to gaze upon God from time to time. And finally, we must finish all our actions looking to God. As time and much labor are necessary to acquire this practice, we must not be discouraged when we fail in it, because the habit is formed only with difficulty; but when it is formed, everything we do we will do with pleasure.

Is it not right that the heart, which is the first member to be quickened to life in us, and which dominates over the other members of our body, should be the first and the last part of us to love and worship God, as we begin or end our spiritual and bodily actions? It is in the heart that we should carefully produce this brief interior glance, which we must do, as I have said before, without struggling or studying to make it easier.

Fourth. It would not be out of place for those who are beginning this practice to inwardly form a few words. We could say, "My God, I am entirely yours; God of love, I love You with all my heart; Lord, do with me according to Your heart," or some other words that love produces spontaneously. But those who are beginning should be wary lest their minds should stray and return to the creature when they should be keeping them on God alone. When their minds are pressed in this way and constrained by their wills, they will be forced to remain with God.

Fifth. Practicing the presence of God is a little difficult in the beginning, but when it is done faithfully, it secretly works marvelous effects in the soul, brings a flood of graces from the Lord, and leads it without its knowledge to gaze simply and lovingly at God and find His presence everywhere. This gaze is the easiest, the most holy, the most solid, and the most effective type of prayer.

Sixth. Please notice that to arrive at this state, we have to mortify our senses, since it is impossible for a soul that still has some creature satisfaction, to fully enjoy this divine presence. To be with God, one must absolutely leave all created things behind.

SIX

The Usefulness of Practicing the Presence of God

First. The first useful thing that the soul receives from practicing the presence of God is a faith that is more alive and more active in every aspect of our lives, particularly in our areas of need. Living this way easily obtains grace for us in our temptations and in the inevitable contact we have with created things. The soul that is accustomed to exercising its faith through this practice sees and feels God's presence by simply remembering God. It invokes Him easily and effectively, and obtains what it needs. By doing this it somewhat approaches the state of those who are already enjoying God's presence in heaven. The more it advances, the more its faith becomes alive, and finally its faith becomes so penetrating that it could almost say, "I no longer *believe*; I *see* and I *experience*."

Second. The practice of the presence of God strengthens our hope. Our hope increases as our spiritual knowledge increases, as our faith lays hold of the very secrets of God. By finding in God a beauty surpassing not only physical bodies on earth, but the beauty of the most perfect souls and of angels, our hope is strengthened. It is reassured by the very greatness of the blessing to which it aspires and that it sometimes actually foretastes.

Third. Practicing the presence of God inspires in the will a disdain of created things, and sets it ablaze with the fire of sacred love. Being always with God who is a consuming fire, this fire of sacred love reduces to ashes all that can be opposed to it. The soul, so kindled, can no longer live except in the presence of its God. This divine presence produces in the heart a holy ardor, a sacred zeal, and a passionate desire to see God loved, known, served, and worshiped by all creation.

Fourth. By practicing the presence of God and by gazing inwardly at Him, the soul so familiarizes itself with God that it spends almost all its life in continual acts of love, adoration, contrition, confidence, thanksgiving, offering, beseeching, and all other excellent virtues. All these acts may even sometimes merge to become nothing less than one single continuing act that no longer comes and goes, because the soul is always in God's divine presence.

I know that there are few people who arrive at this stage; it is a special grace with which God favors only a few chosen souls, since in the end this steady, simple gaze is a gift from His generous hand. But I will say for the consolation of those who wish to embrace this holy practice, that He ordinarily gives this gift to souls who prepare themselves for it. If He does not give it, we can at least, with the help of His ordinary grace, acquire by the practice of the presence of God a state of prayer that comes very close to this simple, continual vision of God.

ST. ANTONY OF EGYPT

From from *The Wisdom of the Desert Fathers and Mothers*

TAKE NO PRIDE IN YOUR FAITHFULNESS

From "The Life of St. Antony"
by St. Athanasius the Great, in *The Wisdom of the Desert Fathers and Mothers*, chapters 1–21

LIFE OF ANTONY

1 Antony, then, came from Egypt; he was the son of well-born and devout parents. He was brought up so carefully by his family that he knew nothing apart from his parents and his home. While he was still a boy, he refused to learn to read and write or to join in the silly games of the other little children. Instead, he burned with a desire for God and lived a life of simplicity at home, as the Bible says of Jacob. He also often went with his parents to church but did not fool around as little children tend to, nor did he show a lack of respect as young boys often do. He concentrated on what was being read and put the useful precepts into practice in his way of life. He was never a nuisance to his family, as children usually are because of their desire for a variety of dainty foods. He did not long for the pleasures of more delicate food; he was content with just what he was given and asked for nothing more.

2 When he and his little sister were left completely on their own after their parents died (Antony was around eighteen

years old), he took good care of his house and his sister. Before six months had passed, though, he was on his way to church one day when he thought about how the apostles had rejected everything to follow the Savior. He thought about how the early Christians had sold their possessions and laid the proceeds at the apostles' feet to distribute to the needy. What great hope was stored up for those people in heaven! As he was thinking about these things, Antony entered the church. As he went into the church, he heard this Gospel being read: *If you wish to be perfect, go, sell your possessions and give the money to the poor, and you will have treasure in heaven; then come, follow me* (Matthew 19:21).

When he heard this, Antony applied the Lord's commandment to himself, believing that because of divine inspiration he had first remembered the incident and that this Scripture was being read aloud for his sake. He immediately went home and sold the possessions he owned. He possessed 300 fertile acres that he shared among his neighbors to prevent anyone from bearing a grudge against him or his sister. All the rest of his possessions, which were movable goods, he sold. The great profit he made from the sale of these goods he gave to the poor. He kept a little for his sister's sake, because she seemed more vulnerable on account of her youth.

3 On another occasion when Antony had gone to church and heard the Lord saying in the Gospel: *Do not worry about tomorrow, for tomorrow will bring worries of its own* (Matthew 6:34), he shared all the rest of his wealth with the poor. He was not content to stay at home, but he left his sister to be brought up by some faithful and good women.

Now free from all worldly ties, he entered into a harsh and severe life. There were not yet many monasteries in Egypt at the time, and there was no one who was familiar with the remote desert. People who wanted to serve Christ settled at a distance from their own villages. On a neighboring estate there was an old man who had lived a solitary life since his youth. When Antony saw this old man, Antony wanted more than anything to imitate the man's goodness. When he started out, Antony lived in places that were not too far from his home. Later, though, whenever he heard about someone who was engaged in this disciplined life, Antony would go out and search for him. He would not return home until he had seen the person he longed to see. After he began in this way, his resolve grew stronger every day until he reached the point where he no longer thought of his family wealth or of his relatives. He focused his desire and his attention on the task he had undertaken, and worked with his hands. For he knew that the Bible teaches that anyone unwilling to work should not eat. Apart from what he needed for bread, the money he earned he gave to the poor. He prayed often, for he had learned that he should pray to the Lord constantly. He also listened intently to the Scriptures so that none of its lessons would be lost on him. He preserved all the Lord's commandments in his memory.

He led his life in such a way that all the brothers loved him with a pure love. He obeyed everyone whom he visited. Eager to learn, he assimilated their various individual gifts. He imitated the self-restraint of one, the cheerfulness of another. He emulated the gentleness of one, the nocturnal devotions of another, and the dedication in reading of yet another. He admired one who fasted and another who slept on the bare ground, praising the endurance of the former and the compassion of the latter. He kept in mind the love they all showed one another, and he returned to his own place refreshed by every aspect of their virtues. There he would ponder all he had learned and try to imitate the good points of each one. He was never provoked to anger. The only fire that burned in his heart was his determination to excel in the deeds just mentioned. He did this in such a way that he was dear to them all, even though he surpassed them in glory. When his neighbors and those monks whom he visited often saw him, they called him God's friend. Some loved him as a son; others loved him as a brother.

5 While Antony was busy with doing all these things that caused so many to love him, the devil, who could not bear to see a young man with such outstanding virtues, began to attack him. First, he tried to drag Antony away from the life to which he had committed himself. He made Antony remember his wealth, his sister's protection, and his family's social status. The devil tried to stimulate in Antony a desire for material things, the short-lived honors of this world, the pleasures of different kinds of food, and many other attractions that belong to an indulgent life. He reminded Antony of the great difficulty in obtaining the life of virtue. He also reminded him of the body's weakness. He created great confusion in Antony's thoughts, hoping to call him back from his intentions. But when, as result of Antony's prayers to God, the devil realized that he had been driven out by Antony's faith in Christ's

sufferings, he seized the weapons with which he normally attacks all young people, using seductive dreams to disturb Antony. First he tried to unsettle him at night by means of hostile hordes and terrifying sounds, and then he attacked him by day with weapons that were so obviously his that no one could doubt that Antony was fighting against the devil. For the devil tried to implant dirty thoughts, but Antony pushed them away by means of constant prayer. The devil tried to titillate his senses by means of natural carnal desires, but Antony defended his whole body by faith, by praying at night, and by fasting. At night the devil would turn himself into the attractive form of a beautiful woman, omitting no detail that might provoke lascivious thoughts, but Antony called to mind the fiery punishment of hell. In this way he resisted the onslaught of lust. The devil without hesitation set before him the slippery path of youth that leads to disaster, but Antony concentrated on the everlasting torments of future judgment and kept his soul's purity untainted throughout these temptations. All these things confounded the devil. A young man was now tricking this evil creature who thought he could become God's equal, as if the devil himself were a wretched creature. A man made of flesh defeated the devil, who tries to defeat flesh and blood. The Lord, who became flesh for our sake and thus granted the body victory over the devil, was helping Antony.

6 At last the devil found he was unable to destroy Antony and that Antony's thoughts were always driving him back. So, crying and gnashing his teeth, he appeared to Antony in a form appropriate to his nature. An ugly dark boy threw himself down at Antony's feet, weeping loudly and saying in a human voice, "I have led many astray, and I have deceived many, but you have defeated my efforts, just as other holy people have done." When Antony asked him who was saying this, the devil replied, "I am the friend of sin. I have used many different kinds of shameful weapons to attack young people, and that is why I am called the spirit of sinfulness. How many of those who were determined to live chastely have I tricked! How many times have I persuaded those starting out hesitantly to return to their former foul ways. I am the one who caused the prophet to reproach the fallen, saying, *The spirit of sinfulness has led you astray* (cf. Hosea 4:12), and I am the one who made them fall. I am the one who has often tempted you, and always you have driven me away." When the soldier of Christ heard this, he gave thanks to God and, strengthened by greater confidence in the face of the enemy, he said, "You are utterly despicable and contemptible; your blackness and your age are signs of weakness. You do not worry me any longer. *The Lord is on my side to help me; I shall look in triumph on those who hate me"* (Psalm 118:7). At the sound of Antony's singing, the apparition immediately vanished.

7 This was Antony's first victory over the devil. It was the first sign of the Savior's power in Antony. The Savior *condemned sin in the flesh, so that the just requirement of the law might be fulfilled in us, who walk not according to the flesh but according to the Spirit* (Romans 8:4). But this triumph did give Antony a sense of security. The devil's powers did not fail completely. The devil, like a roaring lion, was always watching for some way to pounce on Antony. Knowing from the Bible that the devil's wiles are numerous, Antony kept his commitment

firm by skillful effort. Antony realized that although Satan had been defeated in the struggles of the flesh, he could use new strategies and more deadly weapons against him. Thus Antony disciplined his body more and more, afraid that he, who had won some contests, might lose others. He thus began to live a more rigorous rule of life. Even though everyone was amazed at this young man's tireless dedication, Antony endured his discipline patiently because he knew that voluntary servitude to God would transform habit into nature.

8 Antony so endured hunger and sleeplessness that his powers were considered astonishing. He very often spent the entire night in prayer and ate only once a day, after sunset. Sometimes he continued fasting for two or three days at a time and only ate and drank on the fourth day. He ate bread and salt, and drank a little water. I think it is better not to say anything about his consumption of meat and wine, for most monks do not consume either one. When he did allow himself to rest, he used a woven rush mat covered with goats' hair. Sometimes he would simply lie on the bare ground, and he refused to anoint his body with oil. For he used to say that it is hardly possible that the bodies of those who use such things, and especially young men's bodies, should grow strong if they are softened by smooth oil. Instead they ought to use rigorous exercises to control the flesh, as the Apostle Paul said: *Therefore I am content with weaknesses, insults, hardships, persecutions, and calamities for the sake of Christ; for whenever I am weak, then I am strong* (2 Corinthians 12:10). Antony also stated that wearing down the body's energies in this way could revive a person's mental powers. That is the reason he did not measure the value of his tasks by the length of time spent, but with the love and willing servitude characteristic of a novice. He continued to maintain his desire to progress in the fear of God. Wanting to add new achievements to the old ones, he kept in mind Paul's words: *Forgetting what lies behind and straining forward to what lies ahead, I press on toward the goal for the prize of the heavenly call of God in Christ Jesus* (Philippians 3:13). He remembered also what Elijah said: *As the Lord of hosts lives, before whom I stand, I will surely show myself to him today* (1 Kings 18:15). Antony explained that "today" did not mean just past time but that every day he was entering battle, and he wanted to prove himself worthy in God's sight, pure of heart, and ready to obey God's will.

9 Then the holy Antony, bearing in mind that a servant of God should organize his life based on the life of the great Elijah, moved away to some tombs not far from his own village. He asked one of his friends to bring him food at regular intervals. When this brother had shut him up in one of the tombs, Antony remained there alone. But the devil was afraid that the desert might become inhabited because of Antony, so he gathered his followers and tortured Antony by beating him all over. The intensity of the pain deprived Antony of his ability to move and speak. At a later time he would tell how his injuries had been so serious that they were worse than all the tortures devised by other men. However, God's providence saved him. The next day the brother arrived with food as usual and found the tomb's door smashed down and Antony lying half-dead on the ground. He lifted him on his shoulders and carried him back to his house in the village.

When people heard about this, many neighbors and relatives came running and in their grief performed the funeral rites for Antony. When the night was half over, a deep weariness overcame those keeping watch. Then Antony, his spirit gradually returning, drew a deep breath and lifted his head. When he saw that the man who had brought him there was awake while all the others were lying fast asleep, he beckoned to the man and begged him to carry him back, without waking anyone at all, to the place where he had been living.

10 So Antony was carried back to his tomb, and stayed there alone as he had before. Since he could not stand up because of his recent beatings, he prayed lying down. After praying, Antony would say in a loud voice, "Look, here I am. I don't run away from fighting with you. Even if you bring me more difficulties, you cannot separate me from Christ's love." And he would then chant these words: *Though an army encamp against me, my heart shall not fear* (Psalm 27:3). When he heard this, the devil was amazed that Antony had dared to come back. The devil was furious. Gathering his dogs together, he said to them, "See how Antony is overcome neither by the spirit of sinfulness nor by physical pain. To top it all off, he is disrespectful in his challenges to us. Take up all your weapons; we must attack with greater force. Let him feel, let him feel; he must understand who it is that he is provoking." When the devil spoke, all those listening to him agreed with him, for the devil has immeasurable ways of doing harm. Then there was a sudden noise that caused the place to shake violently. Holes appeared in the wall, and a swarm of different kinds of demons poured out. They took on the shape of wild animals and snakes, and instantly they filled the whole place with apparitions in the form of lions, bulls, wolves, vipers, serpents, scorpions, leopards, and bears. They each made noises according to their individual natures: The lion roared, eager for the kill; the bull bellowed and made menacing movements with his horns; the serpent hissed; the wolves leaped forward to attack; the spotted leopard showed all the different wiles of the one that controlled him. Each of their faces bore a savage expression, and the sound of their voices was terrifying. Mauled and beaten, Antony experienced even more atrocious pains in his body; but he remained unafraid, and his mind was alert. Although the wounds of his flesh made him groan, he maintained the same attitude and spoke as if mocking his enemies: "If you had any power, one of you would be enough for the fight; but since the Lord has robbed you of your strength, you are broken and so you attempt to use large numbers to terrify me. The proof of your weakness is that you have taken on the shapes of unreasoning beasts." He continued to speak with confidence: "If you truly have any influence, if the Lord has granted you any power over me, here I am: Eat me up. But if you cannot, why do you use up so much energy? For the sign of the cross and faith in the Lord is for us a wall that no assault of yours can break down." Although they made numerous threats against the holy Antony, they did not succeed. They made fools of themselves, not of Antony.

22 Jesus did not fail to notice his servant's struggle. He came to protect Antony. When Antony raised his eyes, he saw the roof opening above him. As the darkness dissipated, a ray of light poured in on him. As soon as this bright light appeared, all the demons vanished, and the pain in Antony's body suddenly stopped. The building that had been destroyed was restored. Antony immediately understood that the Lord was present. Sighing deeply from the bottom of his heart, he spoke to the light that had appeared to him: "Where were you, good Jesus? Where were you? Why weren't you here from the beginning to heal my wounds?" And a voice came to him: "Antony, I was here, but I was waiting to watch your struggle. But now, since you have bravely held your own in this fight, I will always help you and I will make you famous throughout the world." When he heard this, Antony stood up and prayed; he felt so greatly strengthened that he realized he had received more strength now than he had before he lost it. Antony was thirty-five years old when this happened.

12 Later, as his willing commitment caused him to grow in spiritual goodness, he went to the old man I mentioned earlier and begged that they should live together in the desert. When the old man refused, giving as his excuse his old age and the novelty of the plan, Antony went forth to the mountain alone, having lost all fear of that way of life, and attempted to open up a path to the desert that had before now been unknown to the monks. However, not even there did his tireless adversary give up. Determined to obstruct Antony's commitment to this way of life, the devil threw down a silver plate in his path. When Antony saw it, he recognized the cunning of that ingenious trickster. He stood still and fearless, and, looking at the plate grimly, he rebuked the one trying to trick him with the illusion of silver. He said to himself, "Why is this plate here

in the desert? This track is remote and there are no traces of any travelers. If it had fallen out of someone's luggage, it could hardly have lain unnoticed, for it is too large. If the person who lost it came back, he would certainly have found what had fallen out because this place is so empty. This is a product of your cunning, you devil, but you will not hinder my intention. May your silver plate go to hell with you." As soon as Antony said this, the plate disappeared like smoke from the face of the fire.

13 Next Antony saw a piece of real gold lying in his path. It is not clear whether the devil put it there to deceive him, or whether God revealed it to prove that Antony could not be seduced even by real riches. Antony marveled at the size of this piece of shining metal and quickly ran all the way to the mountain, as if he were escaping from a fire. After crossing the river, he found a deserted fort full of venomous animals. He settled in the fort as its new tenant. Immediately on his arrival, a huge number of snakes fled as if they had been chased out. Antony then blocked up the entrance with stones and stayed there all alone, storing up enough bread for six months as well as a small supply of water. He did not go out to receive any visitors. Even when he took his bread supply through the roof twice a year, he did not talk with those who brought it to him.

14 When crowds of people spent the night outside his door so they could question him, they heard noisy voices as if a number of people were saying to Antony, "Why have you moved into our home? What have you got to do with the desert? Leave other people's property alone. You cannot live here; you cannot endure our attacks." At first those outside thought some people had entered the walls and were quarreling with Antony. But when they looked in through the gaps, they saw no one and realized demons were fighting Antony. They were terribly frightened and called to Antony for help. He came to the door to comfort the brothers; he begged them not to be afraid and asked them to go away. He assured them that their fear was caused by the demons. "Make the sign of the cross," he said, "and leave without fear. Leave these demons to mock themselves." So the people returned to their homes while Antony remained there unharmed, never tiring in his struggle. For he increased in his commitment, and the weakness of his opponents accorded him the greatest relief in his fight and made him steadfast of mind. When crowds of people came to the desert again, they expected to find him dead. But he sang from within, *Let God rise up, let his enemies be scattered; let those who hate him flee before him. As smoke is driven away, so drive them away; as wax melts before the fire, let the wicked perish before God* (Psalm 68:1–2). He also sang, *All nations surrounded me; in the name of the Lord I cut them off!* (Psalm 118:10).

15 Antony spent twenty years in the desert in this way, staying out of humankind's sight. Many came to see him in their desire to imitate his commitment to his way of life. A number of people who were suffering also gathered outside his door. When they at last managed to tear down the doors by force, Antony appeared to them with an aura of holiness as if he had emerged from some divine sanctuary. Everyone was stunned at the beauty of his expression and the dignified bearing of his body, which had not grown weak through lack of exercise. His face had not grown pale as the result of fasting and fighting with demons. To the contrary, his body looked as if no time had passed. What a great miracle. What purity of mind he had. Never did excessive frivolity cause him to burst out laughing; never did the thought of past sins make him frown, nor did the high praise bestowed on him by his admirers make him conceited. The solitude had in no way made him uncivilized, and the daily battles with his enemies had not brutalized him. His mind was calm, and he maintained a well-balanced attitude in all situations. Then the grace of God, through Antony, freed many people from unclean spirits and from various illnesses. His speech brought comfort to those who were grieving, instructed the ignorant, reconciled those who were angry, and persuaded everyone that nothing should be valued higher than Christ's love. He set before their eyes the great number of future rewards as well as the mercy of God, and he made known the benefits granted because God did not spare His own Son but had given him for the salvation of us all. His words had the immediate effect of persuading many of those who heard him to reject human things. This was the beginning of the colonization of the desert.

16 I should also mention what happened in the region of Arsinoe. Antony planned to visit the brothers there. He had to swim across the Nile River, which was full of crocodiles and other dangerous animals. He and his companions crossed the river without harm and returned safely, too. After that he continued steadfastly in his ascetic efforts, and he inspired many of the brothers by his teaching. In a short

time a large number of monastic prayer chambers came into existence. He guided these monks with a fatherly affection.
17 One day, when the brothers who had gathered there were asking the holy Antony to provide some guidelines for their way of life, he raised his voice with a prophet's confidence and said that the Scriptures were sufficient for all teaching of the rule. He taught also that it would be an excellent idea for the brothers to support each other with mutual encouragement. "And so," he said, "you should tell me, as if I were your father, what you have learned, and I will reveal to you, as if you were my sons, what I have discovered as a result of my great age. But let this be the first rule, shared by all of you, that no one should weaken in the firmness of his commitment to the way of life he has chosen. He should strive always to increase his commitment to this undertaking as if he were just starting out, especially because human life, compared to eternity, is very short." After beginning in this way, Antony was silent for a while. Marveling at God's great generosity, he then added, "In this present life, things of equal value are exchanged: The seller does not receive more from the buyer. But the promise of eternal life is brought at a low price. As it is written: *The days of our life are seventy years, or perhaps eighty if we are strong; even then their span is only toil and trouble; they are soon gone, and we fly away* (Psalm 90:10). If we have lived in God's work for eighty or a hundred years, working hard, we will not reign for the same amount of time in the future. Instead, in exchange for the years I mentioned, we shall be granted a reign lasting throughout all ages. It is not earth that we will inherit, but

heaven. We shall leave this corrupt body and we shall receive it incorrupt.

18 "And so, my children, do not let yourselves grow weary. Do not be seduced by pride in your achievement. *For the sufferings of this present time are not worth comparing with the glory about to be revealed to us* (Romans 8:18). No one, once he has rejected this world, should think he has left behind anything important. The entire earth, compared to the infinity of the heavens, is small and limited. Even if we renounce the whole world, we cannot give anything in exchange that is of similar value to the heavenly dwellings. If each person considers this, he will immediately realize that if he abandons a few acres of land or a small house or a moderate sum of gold, he ought not to feel proud of himself in the belief that he has given up a lot. Nor should he become despondent, thinking that he will receive only a little in return. For just as someone considers one dollar of no value in comparison with winning one hundred dollars, so, too, anyone who renounces possession of the entire world will receive in heaven a hundred times as much in more valuable rewards. In short, we must realize that even if we want to retain our riches, we will be torn away from them against our will by the law of death, as it says in Ecclesiastes. Why then do we not make a virtue of necessity? Why do we not voluntarily abandon what must be destroyed when this light comes to an end, so that we might gain the kingdom of heaven? Let Christians care for nothing that they cannot take away with them. We ought rather to seek after that which will lead us to heaven, namely wisdom, chastity,

justice, virtue, an ever-watchful mind, care of the poor, firm faith in Christ, a mind that can control anger, and hospitality. Striving after these things, we shall prepare for ourselves a dwelling in the land of the peaceful, as it says in the Gospel.

19 "Let us bear in mind that we are servants of the Lord and that we owe a service to him who created us. For a servant does not reject present or future authority on account of past service, and does not dare to claim that because of his past he ought to be released from the task at hand. Instead, he continues to perform the same service with unbroken commitment so as to please his master and so that his wages will not be fear and beatings. In the same way it is right for us to obey the divine commandments, knowing that he who is a just judge will judge each person where he finds him, as the prophet Ezekiel testifies. Even the wretched Judas, because of one night's sins, lost out on the rewards for all his past achievement.

20 "We must therefore be steadily committed to this way of life with God as our helper, for it is written: *We know that all things work together for good for those who love God* (Romans 8:28). Let us reflect on the Apostle's claim that he dies each day, so that we can avoid idleness. If we bear in mind the unpredictability of our human condition, we will not sin. For when we wake from sleep, we are unsure whether we will reach evening, and when we lie down to rest at night, we should not be confident that daylight will return. We should be aware always of the uncertainty of our life and know that we are governed by God's providence. Not only will we not go astray nor be swept away by some flimsy desire, but neither

will we be angry with anyone nor strive to accumulate earthly treasures. Instead, fearing death each day and always thinking about our separation from the body, we will trample upon all that is transitory. The desire for women will disappear, the fire of lust will be extinguished, and we will pay our debts to each other, always holding before our eyes the coming of the final retribution. For a powerful fear of judgment and a terrible dread of punishment destroy the incentives of the lustful flesh and support the soul as it slips off the cliff's edge.

21 "I pray then that we should use every effort to press on toward this life's goal. Let no one look behind him as did Lot's wife, especially since the Lord has said that no one who puts his hand upon the plough and looks back is fit for the kingdom of heaven. To look back means to have second thoughts about your undertaking and to become entangled once more in worldly desires. Do not fear the word 'virtue' as if it were unattainable. Do not think that such an endeavor, which depends on our will, is alien to you or something remote. Man has a natural inclination to this kind of effort, and it is something that awaits only our willingness. Let the Greeks pursue their studies across the seas and go in search of teachers of useless literature in foreign lands. We, however, feel no compulsion to travel across the waves, for the kingdom of heaven is to be found everywhere on earth. That is why the Lord says in the Gospel: *The kingdom of God is among you* (Luke 17:21). The virtue that is within us requires only the human will. For who can doubt that the natural purity of the soul, were it not tainted by filth, would be the source of all virtues? A good Creator must necessarily have

made the soul good. If we hesitate, we should hear the words of Joshua, who said, *Incline your hearts to the LORD, the God of Israel* (Joshua 24:33). And John expresses a similar idea about virtue when he says, *Make his paths straight* (Matthew 3:3). For to have a straight soul means that the blemish of any vices does not stain its original soundness. If it changes its nature, then it is said to have gone astray, but if it preserves its good nature, then that is virtue. The Lord has entrusted our soul to us: Let us keep what has been entrusted to us in the same state as it was in when we received it. No one can put forward as an excuse that what is born in him is external to him. Let him who made us recognize his own creation, and let him find his own work as he created it. Our natural adornment is enough for us: You who are human must not disfigure what divine generosity has granted you. To wish to alter the works of God is to desecrate them.

22 "We ought to be careful to ensure that we control the tyrannical passion of anger, since it says in the Bible, *Your anger does not produce God's righteousness* (James 1:20), and *Desire gives birth to sin, and that sin, when fully grown, gives birth to death* (James 1:15). The divine voice has recommended that we should protect our soul with unceasing vigilance and lead it toward perfection with all care and effort, because we have enemies who are trained to trip us up. These are the demons whom we must fight without a truce, according to the testimony of the Apostle who says: *For our struggle is not against enemies of flesh and blood, but against the rulers, against the authorities, against the cosmic powers of this present darkness, against the spiritual forces of evil in the heavenly places*

(Ephesians 6:12). Huge numbers of them are flying through the air here; the enemy troops are rushing all around us. I am not able to describe their diversity, so I shall leave this task to those who are more competent than I. I shall give a brief account, though, of the things one should be aware of, specifically the tricks the demons have devised against us.

23 "First of all, we should hold firm in our minds the fact that God has made nothing that is evil and that the demons did not derive their origin from any arrangement on his part."

SPIRITUAL MAXIMS ON PRIDE AND HUMILITY

St. Antony of Egypt, from *The Wisdom of the Desert Fathers and Mothers*

SAYINGS OF THE FATHERS AND MOTHERS

Antony the Great

2 When Antony thought about the depth of God's judgments, he asked, "Lord, how is it that some die when they are young, while others drag on to extreme old age? Why are there those who are poor and those who are rich? Why do wicked men prosper, and why are the just in need?" He heard a voice answering him, "Antony, keep your attention on yourself; these things happen according to God's judgment, and it is not to your advantage to know anything about them."

3 Someone asked Antony, "What must one do in order to please God?" He replied, "Pay attention to what I tell you. Whoever you may be, always have God before your eyes. Whatever you do, do it according to the testimony of the holy Scriptures. Wherever you live, do not easily leave it. Keep these three precepts and you will be saved."

4 Father Antony said, "This is the great work of a person: always to take the blame for his or her own sins before God and to expect temptation until the last breath."

6 Father Pambo asked Father Antony, "What ought I to do?" Antony replied, "Do not trust in your own righteousness, do not worry about the past, but control your tongue and your stomach."

10 Antony said, "Just as fish die if they stay too long out of water, so the monks who loiter outside their prayer chambers or pass their time with men of the world lose the intensity of their inner peace. So, like a fish going toward the sea, we must hurry to reach our prayer chamber. If we delay outside, we will lose our interior watchfulness."

15 The brothers praised a monk before Antony. When the monk came to see him, Antony wanted to know how he would bear insults. Seeing that he could not bear them at all, Antony said to him, "You are like a village magnificently decorated on the outside, but destroyed from within by robbers."

30 Some say that the Holy Spirit carried Antony along, but he would never talk about this with men. Such men see what is happening in the world, as well as knowing what is going to happen.

31 One day Antony received a letter from Constantine asking him to come to Constantinople. He wondered whether he ought to go, and he asked his disciple his thoughts. The follower said, "If you go, you will be called simply Antony, but if you stay here you will be called Father Antony."

32 Antony said, "I no longer fear God, but I love him. For love casts out fear."

33 He also said, "Always have the fear of God before your eyes. Remember him who gives death and life. Hate the world and all that is in it. Hate all peace that comes from the flesh. Renounce this life, so that you may be alive to God. Remember what you have promised God, for it will be required of you on the day of judgment. Suffer hunger, thirst, nakedness; be watchful and sorrowful; weep, and groan in your heart; test yourselves, to see if you are worthy of God; despise the flesh, so that you may preserve your souls."

35 Antony said, "Whoever hammers a lump of iron, first decides what he is going to make from it. Even so we ought to make up our minds what kind of virtue we want to forge, or we labor in vain."

37 He also said, "Nine monks fell away after many labors and were obsessed with spiritual pride. They put their trust in their own works. So deceived, they did not heed properly the commandment that says, 'Ask your father and he will tell you.'"

ST. CATHERINE OF SIENA

From *Little Talks with God*

PERSEVERE IN HUMBLE PRAYER

From "The Life of St. Antony"
by St. Athanasius the Great, in *The Wisdom of the Desert Fathers and Mothers*, chapters 1–21

*How a servant of God,
elevated by her desire for God's honor
and for the salvation of her neighbors,
after she had seen the union of the soul with
God, exerted herself in humble prayer and
asked of God four requests.*

When the soul is lifted by a great, yearning desire for the honor of God and the salvation of souls, it practices the ordinary virtues and remains in the cell of self-knowledge, so that it may know better God's goodness toward it. It does this because knowledge must come before love, and only when it has attained love can it strive to follow and to clothe itself with the truth.

But humble and continuous prayer, founded on knowledge of oneself and of God, is the best way for the creature to receive such a taste of the truth. Following the footprints of Christ crucified, and through humble and unceasing prayer, the soul is united with God. He remakes it in his image through desire, affection, and union of love. Christ seems to have meant this when he said: Those who keep my commandments are the ones who love me, and I will reveal myself to them; they shall be one with me and I one with them. In several places we find similar words, by which we can see that the soul becomes another Himself through the effect of love.

So you may see this more clearly, I will mention a story that a servant of God told me. When she was exalted in prayer, God did not conceal from her the love that he has for his servants. Instead, he revealed that love, saying to her, "Open the eye of your intellect and gaze into me, and you shall see the beauty of my rational creature. Look at those creatures whom I have created in my image and likeness, and have clothed with the wedding garment of love and adorned with many virtues, by which they are united with me through love. Yet if you should ask me who these are, I should reply," said the gentle and loving Word of God, "they are another me, for they have lost and denied their own will, and they are clothed, united, and conformed to my will." It is therefore true that the soul is united with God through love's affection.

So this servant of God, who wanted to know and follow the truth more faithfully, addressed four requests to the supreme and eternal Father. First, she prayed for herself, for this servant believed that she could not be an example to her neighbor in matters of doctrine and prayer if she did not first obtain her own virtue. Her second prayer was for the reformation of the holy church. The third was a general prayer for the entire world, particularly for the peace of Christians who rebel against and persecute the holy church. In the fourth prayer she asked for divine providence to sustain the world, and to be active in a certain case with which she was concerned.

NOTES

Notes for Book I of *The Imitation of Christ*

1. 1 John 8:12.
2. Revelation 2:17.
3. Acts 10:35.
4. Ecclesiastes 1:2, Deuteronomy 6:13.
5. Matthew 6:33.
6. Matthew 6:19–20.
7. Ecclesiastes 1:8.
8. 2 Corinthians 4:18.
9. Hebrews 12:15, 2 Peter 2:10.
10. Aristotle, *Metaphysics*, I, 1.
11. Matthew 7:21, 1 Corinthians 13:2.
12. 1 Timothy 3:9.
13. Romans 11:20.
14. Romans 12:16.
15. *Ama nesciri* (Love to be unknown) is quoted from St. Bernard. It was a favorite phrase among the Brethren of the Common Life. We are told that this entire sentence appears in another work of à Kempis, *The Little Alphabet of a Monk.*
16. *Inordinate:* not kept within bounds, immoderate, unrestrained, excessive. This word implies the exceeding of bounds prescribed by authority or dictated by good judgment. It appears often in this work, but is not a word in common use today.
17. Psalm 31:1.
18. Jeremiah 9:23.
19. James 4:6.
20. Psalm 131:1–2.
21. Matthew 5:8.
22. 1 Corinthians 10:13.

23. John 6:63.
24. Psalm 94:12–13.
25. See Isaiah 23:4.
26. Romans 7:24.
27. Revelation 2:23; Matthew 5:6, 25:21.
28. See John 12:48.
29. Psalm 69:17.
30. Psalm 143:10.
31. Genesis 17:1.
32. John 8:31.
33. 1 Corinthians 4:7.
34. Matthew 26:39, John 5:30, 6:38.
35. 1 Corinthians 10:24.
36. Luke 14:10.
37. Matthew 6:10.
38. Matthew 5:48.
39. Psalm 71:12.
40. Isaiah 14:2–3.
41. Psalm 43:3.
42. John 21:22.
43. 1 Peter 4:7.
44. John 14:27.
45. Matthew 6:22.
46. Exodus 18:18, Micah 4:9.
47. Psalm 51:12.
48. Ephesians 3:16.
49. Matthew 6:34.
50. Ecclesiastes 1:14, 2:1.
51. Ephesians 4:14.

BRIEF BIOGRAPHIES OF THE CONTRIBUTORS

THOMAS À KEMPIS
CA. 1380–1471

Thomas Hammerken was born in 1380 in Kempin, a small, walled town near Cologne, Germany. His brother John, fifteen years his senior, went early into the religious life. When Thomas was twelve, he went at his brother's advice to Deventer, where Florentius received him and provided schooling, housing, books, and board for the next seven years. He attended the village school, run by the brothers, sang in the choir, and "learned to write," joining the noble copyists at their work.

After his training at Deventer, Thomas went in 1399, with Florentius's blessing, to Mount St. Agnes, the first daughterhouse of Windesheim, where his brother John had been cofounder and was now prior. Florentius sent a request that the rule against having two brothers in the same monastery be set aside in their case, and it was done. Here Thomas spent the rest of his long life. He waited six years before becoming a novice, and on June 10, 1406, he made his solemn profession as an Augustinian Canon Regular. Seven more years would pass before he was ordained, at the age of thirty-three.

Once we hear of his traveling to Windesheim on business. In 1429 he accompanied the rest of the brethren in their migration to Ludenkerk, to avoid the papal interdict that Windesheim suffered as a result of a disputed canonical election. During this absence, Thomas was called away from Ludenkerk to the Convent of Bethany, to care for his dying brother John. Altogether he was away from Mount St. Agnes for about three years out of seventy-two. Twice he was elected sub-prior and once he was procurator [or bursar] of the community. But he was not a good business manager, and he appears to have been glad to return to literary work, training the novices, and meditating in his beloved cell.

It had been the practice of Gerard Groote and Florentius to encourage the brothers to keep a book of extracts from their readings—pithy and meaningful sayings and thoughts gleaned mainly from their reading. Gerard set the example himself, and has, indeed, been credited by some as being the real author of this book. Without doubt, his practice of encouraging the keeping of *raparia,* as these books were called, lies behind the book. Since the *raparia* were kept for the good of all, Thomas would have had access not only to his own book, but also to those of others, greatly expanding the numbers of authors who would become known to him. It is not surprising, therefore, that we find allusions or quotations from St. Augustine, St. Bernard of Clairvaux, St. Francis of Assisi, St. Thomas Aquinas, St. Bonaventura, St. Gregory the Great, and even from such classical authors as Aristotle, Ovid, and Seneca. There are also echoes of medieval Latin hymns, and "you can scarcely read a sentence," said one observer, "that does not recall some passage, now in the Old, now in the New Testament."

"If it be mainly quotation," says Dean Sperry, "it is 'inspired quotation.' It is a single, closely wrought work, wanting perhaps in novelty but marked by profound originality" (Sperry, p. 65).

Apart from his historical sources, even remembrances that the author quotes unconsciously, there is the stamp of immediate inspiration and the spark of fire of a soul that is turned to God and is listening to what the Spirit is saying. When he says, "I will hear what the Lord God will speak in me" (Book III, Chapter 1), we can believe that he means exactly that, and that he is listening in spirit to the inner voice of the Consoler and Strengthener of Christians, the Holy Spirit.

From many references in the *Imitation,* it is obvious that Thomas practiced what he preached. When he expresses concern about those who compete with one another as to whose saint is the greatest, he is undoubtedly letting us glimpse some of the malaise of his time—the competition for honor and prestige among monasteries and convents. But he prefers to leave all honors and preferments to God.

When he talks about those who run about from shrine to shrine, he reflects the fascination for pilgrimage characteristic of his century. But he confesses that he has seldom "gone abroad," meaning outside the monastery, without returning home less a man than he was. And he observes that he sees little fruit or change for the better in the lives of those who busy themselves rushing about to see and hear new things.

When he talks about the need for repentance before God, we can hear the sorrow and grief of his own heart, as he reviews his own sin and unworthiness before the Holy of Holies.

So the book transcends its time, its geographical origins, even its author's individuality, and becomes a document for all times, speaking to the perennial human condition and dealing with the issues of our human need and the transforming power of Jesus Christ. Where others look for a different world, Thomas looks for a different self. His calling is to live each day in simple obedience to the Lord, and to pursue his daily tasks in the knowledge that only a changed heart can result in any lasting change for good. Some critics have criticized him as being essentially self-centered. They should look again at the profound and lasting influence this book has had over the past five hundred years. His words and thoughts have served as a stabilizing ballast for many others who have felt called to a more "active" life in the world and have plunged into the fray, to fight or work for change and progress in other ways.

The Imitation of Christ is a perpetual reminder that action—without humility and without a realistic sense of our human condition—will always in the long run be a "tale full of sound and fury, signifying nothing." On the other hand, this book should be an encouragement to those who seem destined to live out their lives in hidden, unnoticed places, with no great achievements to mark up to their credit, and no lasting fame to attach to their names.

"He shows us," says Kettlewell, "how the life of a Christian in ordinary circumstances may be made lovely by the cultivation of the spiritual life. . . ." That should be justification enough for any book!

BROTHER LAWRENCE
1611–1691

Brother Lawrence of the Resurrection was born Nicholas Herman in the French village of Herimenil in the province of Lorraine in 1611, of poor but pious parents. We know nothing of his schooling, though it could not have been extensive. His language, quoted several times, shows the rusticity of his peasant background, yet this very simplicity makes his wisdom and devotion all the more remarkable, since they always bear the originality and freshness of one who proceeds from inner knowledge, rather than repeating what has been learned from others.

As a young man, Nicholas "had the misfortune of becoming involved" in the military conflict between Lorraine and a neighboring German area. Such conflicts were all too common in Europe at that time. Thinking that he was a spy, the German troops captured Nicholas and threatened him with death. He was able to convince his captors that he was not a spy, and eventually they let him go.

Another armed conflict at this time brought Swedish soldiers into his home province, and in the ensuing battle, Nicholas was wounded. He returned to his parents' home to recover. These two experiences ended whatever taste he had had for the military life.

By his own account, a remarkable spiritual awakening had occurred when he was eighteen years old, about the time he entered military service. De Beaufort's words, dated August 3, 1666, tell it best:

> He told me about his conversion at the age of eighteen before he entered the monastic life. God blessed him with an unusual and remarkable measure of his grace. One winter's day he saw a tree stripped of its leaves, and considered that sometime afterward these leaves would appear again, followed by flowers and fruit. He then received a lofty awareness of the providence and power of God that never left him. This awareness caused him to become entirely detached from the world and gave him such love for God that he could not say whether it had increased during the more than forty years since he had received this gift.

Like every description of an encounter with the living God, words fail to do justice to it. Someone has commented that too many people who had mystical experiences that they admitted were ineffable, would then make the mistake of trying to put them into words. We can take our own inner awakenings, however—those indescribable moments when the heavens seem to open, and we catch a glimpse of something glorious beyond thought or words—and read Brother Lawrence's words in light of them.

After leaving the military life, Nicholas was employed as footman to Monsieur de Fieubet, a prominent banker. A footman was a servant whose duty was to attend the door and the table, and to perform various other tasks. Concerning this time, Brother Lawrence recalled that "he was a clumsy fellow who used to break everything."

The combined period of service in the military and as a footman lasted a number of years. It was one of the frequently remembered regrets in his later life that he did not more quickly leave the world to devote himself entirely to the service of God.

Nonetheless, drawn more and more from the vanity of the age, Nicholas sought counsel from an uncle who was a member of the Carmelite Order. The uncle confirmed his growing conviction that the only safe path was to withdraw entirely from the world and its subtle corruptions. "The air of the world is so contagious," said the uncle, "that if it does not strike dead all who breathe it, it inevitably alters or corrupts the morals of those who follow its ways."

The "ways" of his age were certainly among the most corrupt of history. For this was the age of Louis XIV, the Sun King. Ambitious, vain, and convinced that everything was his by divine right, Louis made almost continuous war a part of his policy. Furthermore, his court was notorious for its immorality, vanity, and worldliness. The palace of Versailles today represents the worldly splendor with which the age was fascinated. In addition, the systematic persecution of Huguenots by the government led to the emigration of 250,000 people. Controversies within the Church stirred passions and resulted in the banishment of the great Archbishop François de Fénelon, who had been chosen earlier as tutor to the King's grandson and heir to the throne, and in the imprisonment of such other souls as Madame Guyon for her supposedly heretical teachings.

Nicholas first sought spiritual surrender in the solitude of a hermit's life. This he was able to do under the tutelage of a gentleman of means, who had himself become weary of the world and was seeking to devote himself fully to the spiritual life, "to taste how sweet the Lord is to those who search for Him with all their heart."

What had proved a blessed state of spiritual fulfillment for some, however, proved to be a place of torment for Nicholas. He found his own emotions running the gamut from joy and peace to sadness and agitation, and from fervor of devotion to complete dryness. It was not long before he realized that the hermit's life was not for him. In 1649, he presented himself as a candidate in the Order of Discalced (Barefooted) Carmelites in Paris.

The Carmelites consisted of lay brothers and brothers in Holy Orders, and their known history goes back to the thirteenth century, when a group of them lived near the well of Elijah the prophet on Mt. Carmel in the Holy Land. They were one of the most austere of monastic communities, devoting themselves to prayer and contemplation. Shortly after the middle of the sixteenth century, a drastic reform had been attempted by St. Teresa of Avila and her disciple St. John of the Cross. Their work was so strongly opposed by the leaders of the Carmelites that ultimately the Order was divided officially between the regular Carmelites, practicing a modified, less severe form of religious life, and the barefooted Carmelites, who sought an even more austere form of self-denial. The refusal to wear shoes was intended to express reverence, humiliation, poverty, and penance, and the brothers wore sandals or went completely barefooted.

In this latter community, Nicholas found the theme that would echo through all his own writings and in those conversations that have been recorded: the absolute negation of everything that does not come from God. In this the Order was following the teaching of St. John of the Cross. The community also put great emphasis on prayer and meditation. Its constitution, drawn up after the division in 1567, prescribed three hours of prayer daily, and one of them, at least, was to be spent "reading aloud the point to be meditated on during the mental prayer that followed."

When he entered the Carmelites, Nicholas was given the name of Lawrence of the Resurrection, by which he would be known to succeeding generations. The practice of giving new names to persons entering the Religious Life has a long history and is still in effect. He says that when he entered, he expected to be "flayed" for his clumsiness, but that instead, "God had fooled him, since he found only satisfaction," and he adds that he often said to God, "You have deceived me!"

In his early days in the Religious Life, he often spent his entire prayer time rejecting stray thoughts and falling back into them again. In fact, he confessed, he had never been able to pray by a rule like the others, and that after the required time of meditation he would not have been able to say what it was about. How easy it is to identify with his difficulty in sustaining a spirit of prayer for a long period!

His solution to this difficulty was a simple one: he developed the habit of continual conversation with God. Whether at prayer or at work, it became his practice to focus his heart and mind on God, thanking Him, praising Him, and asking for His grace to do whatever had to be done. And if he allowed himself to forget God, he confessed that to Him, drawing his thoughts back to God, like wayward children.

Early in his novitiate, he was assigned to work in the monastery kitchen—possibly in recognition of his previous experience as a footman. Far from loving the kitchen, however, he had a natural aversion to it. But since he had determined to do everything for the love of God, he went prayerfully to his tasks, and for some fifteen years "found great ease in doing things" there.

In his later years, he was sent to Auvergne and Burgundy to purchase wine for the community, a task for which he felt totally inadequate. Two factors made the job particularly difficult for him: his lack of skill in business, and the fact that he was so crippled in one leg that he could not walk on the boat except by "rolling himself on the wine casks." Again, he took his case to God, telling Him that it was His business he was embarked on, and after turning it all over to God, "not only was he able to complete his task, but it was done well." Speaking of it later, however, Brother Lawrence said that he did not know how it was done, "that no credit should be given to him at all."

After these assignments, Lawrence was given the task of cobbling shoes, probably in deference to his lameness. In this "he found delight," but professed that he was ready to leave it at any time to do whatever he was asked to do, "doing nothing other than rejoicing everywhere in doing little things for the love of God."

It must not be assumed, however, that life was all smooth and happy for him. He had entered the Religious Life in "great trouble of spirit," absolutely convinced that he was damned. For four years this state of spiritual uncertainty and anxiety stayed with him, and no amount of reasoning or counsel seemed to help. Then came the breakthrough.

Reasoning that he had entered the Religious Order only for the love of God, and that he had been trying to act only for Him, he decided that, whether damned or not, he would continue until death in the same way, trying to do whatever he did out of love for God. This resolution having been firmly established and lived out for a time, he ceased to wonder about heaven or hell, and he found a continual rejoicing and freedom of spirit.

His one concern seems to have been that he did not suffer enough! In his last illness, he did suffer severe pain from pleurisy, but his cheerful countenance so covered it that some of his brothers actually wondered if he was suffering at all.

His counsels, contained in four "conversations" and a brief collection of "Spiritual Maxims" or sayings that were found among his belongings after his death, lift up one theme continually: love for God is everything, and out of that love should proceed a continual internal awareness of God and conversation with Him.

"Although we might do every possible penance," he says, "if our penances are not done in love, they will not serve to erase a single sin." In another place, he notes, "All we must do is recognize God's intimate presence within us and speak to Him at every moment, asking Him for His help. In this way we will know His will in doubtful things and we will do well those things that He is clearly asking of us, offering them to Him before doing them and giving Him thanks for having done them once we have finished."

After his death, his friend and admirer de Beaufort gathered his sayings, together with notes he himself had made of his conversations with Brother Lawrence, and published them for the edification of others. Both Fénelon and Madame Guyon quoted Brother Lawrence at her trial, but their association with the Quietist movement seems to have caused Brother Lawrence's name and influence to fade quickly from the French scene. His words and counsels fell on receptive hearts, however, among English-speaking people, especially Protestants, who continued to publish and read him from that day to this.

In the nineteenth century, the English Quaker Hannah Whitall Smith called *The Practice of the Presence of God* "one of the most helpful books I know." She continued, "It fits into the lives of all human beings, let them be rich or poor, learned or unlearned, wise or simple. The woman at her wash-tub, or the stonebreaker on the road, can carry on the 'practice' here taught with as much ease and as much assurance of success as the priest at his altar or the missionary in his field of work."

ST. ANTONY OF EGYPT
251–356

Perhaps the most famous of the desert fathers was Antony of Egypt, who lived to be 105 years old. Not long after Antony's death, Athanasius, bishop of Alexandria, wrote an account of Antony's life that soon became a model for all other early Christian biographies. Athanasius's book appears to have become an immediate bestseller and to have remained one up through the Middle Ages. In his *Confessions*, Augustine remarks on the power of Athanasius's *Life of Antony*: "They found there a book in which was written the life of Antony. One of them began to read it. He was amazed and set on fire, and during his reading began to think of taking up this way of life and leaving his secular post in the civil service to be your servant."

ST. CATHERINE OF SIENA
1347–1380

Biographers of Catherine have faced great difficulties in reconstructing the life of their subject, because her life is so embedded in legend and piety. In addition, some of the earliest biographies of Catherine were themselves hagiographies, creating a portrait of a pious mystical woman whose transports to God made her an unreachable subject. Even so, there are many facets of Catherine's life of which we can be sure.

Catherine was born in 1347 to a wool dyer in the Fontebranda district of Siena. Caterina di Giacomo di Benincasa, a precocious young girl, was the twenty-fourth of twenty-five children. She was a headstrong and independent child, clever and ingenious in her religious devotion. Catherine's passionate desire for truth and the knowledge of God motivated her very being, even in her youth.

The Dominican Order influenced Catherine greatly. She often visited the church and cloister of San Domenico, a hub of Dominican teaching, spending a great deal of time with these teachers. She was also influenced in Dominican teachings by the brother of her brother-in-law Tommaso della Fonte, who had joined the Dominican order in 1349.

Another group that impressed Catherine was a group of women in Siena known as the *Mantellate*. These women, who wore the habit of the Dominican Order, lived in their homes and ministered to the sick and poor. Even though they did not live in a cloister, they were directed by a prioress. By the time she was fourteen, Catherine had decided not to marry, and she sought and gained entrance to this group of women.

Raymond Capua, her earliest biographer and close friend, records that Catherine vowed her virginity to God when she was just seven years old. At fifteen, she defied her parents and refused their efforts to force her to marry, and at eighteen she obtained the Dominican habit. After she joined the Dominicans, she lived for a period of about three years in silence and solitude, leaving her room only to attend Mass. By the time she was twenty-one, she had experienced her "mystical espousal" to Christ. Soon after she began her work with the Mantellate.

Much like Mother Teresa, Catherine devoted herself to taking care of the sick and indigent. However, during this period of ministering to society, she never gave up her contemplative life, and could often be found at home in her room teaching her followers about the Bible, theology, and God's grace and truth.

In 1370, Catherine had one of her most profound mystical experiences—her "mystical death." For four hours she experienced ecstatic union with God, even though to outside observers she appeared to be dead. This experience led her to become more severe in her self-discipline, and enabled her to have a clear vision of the ways that she could introduce God's truth to the world.

From the time of her "mystical death" to her physical death, Catherine worked tirelessly in political and religious affairs. In 1375, in Pisa, she preached that military strength could be best used to win unbelievers in the Holy Land. She preached that shedding one's blood for Christ was an honorable mission, and so she supported a Crusade through her words. In the same year she received the stigmata, though by her own request these wounds were not visible.

Catherine soon became involved in urging Gregory XI to move the papacy from Avignon back to Rome. During these years she was also active in preaching about clergy reform and martyrdom through Crusades. After Gregory's death, Urban VI replaced him as pope. Because many people opposed Urban when he was elected pope, Catherine foresaw the possibility that schism could occur in the Church. She began a furious letter-writing campaign in order to urge fidelity to the Church. Much of this urging makes its way into her book, *The Dialogue*.

Sometime between 1375 and 1378, Catherine founded a women's monastery outside of Siena in the old fortress of Belcaro. During these years she wrote *The Dialogue*. In this, her most famous writing, she expressed many of her concerns about Church unity, personal austerity and devotion, love of neighbor, clergy reform, God's grace and mercy, and the passionate search for God's truth.

From the time Catherine was thirty until her death at thirty-three, she directed a "household" in Siena where women and men lived by strict observance to poverty and alms. Her final years were filled with physical agony, even though she managed to attend services at Saint Peter's each day. She died on April 29, 1380, and since 1969, the Roman Catholic Church has observed April 29 as her feast day.

ABOUT PARACLETE PRESS

WHO WE ARE

Paraclete Press is a publisher of books, recordings, and DVDs on Christian spirituality. Our publishing represents a full expression of Christian belief and practice—from Catholic to Evangelical, from Protestant to Orthodox.

We are the publishing arm of the Community of Jesus, an ecumenical monastic community in the Benedictine tradition. As such, we are uniquely positioned in the marketplace without connection to a large corporation and with informal relationships to many branches and denominations of faith.

WHAT WE ARE DOING

Books

Paraclete publishes books that show the richness and depth of what it means to be Christian. Although Benedictine spirituality is at the heart of all that we do, we publish books that reflect the Christian experience across many cultures, time periods, and houses of worship. We publish books that nourish the vibrant life of the church and its people—books about spiritual practice, formation, history, ideas, and customs.

We have several different series, including the best-selling Paraclete Essentials and Paraclete Giants series of classic texts in contemporary English; Voices from the Monastery—men and women monastics writing about living a spiritual life today; award-winning poetry; best-selling gift books for children on the occasions of baptism and first communion; and the Active Prayer Series that brings creativity and liveliness to any life of prayer.

Recordings

From Gregorian chant to contemporary American choral works, our music recordings celebrate sacred choral music through the centuries. Paraclete distributes the recordings of the internationally acclaimed choir Gloriæ Dei Cantores, praised for their "rapt and fathomless spiritual intensity" by *American Record Guide*, and the Gloriæ Dei Cantores Schola, which specializes in the study and performance of Gregorian chant. Paraclete is also the exclusive North American distributor of the recordings of the Monastic Choir of St. Peter's Abbey in Solesmes, France, long considered to be a leading authority on Gregorian chant.

Videos

Our videos offer spiritual help, healing, and biblical guidance for life issues: grief and loss, marriage, forgiveness, anger management, facing death, and spiritual formation.

Learn more about us at our website: www.paracletepress.com, or call us toll-free at 1-800-451-5006.

SCAN TO READ MORE

You may also be interested in these Paraclete Essentials . . .

The Imitation of Christ

978-1-55725-608-9 | Trade paper, $15.99

Thomas à Kempis was a late medieval Catholic monk, a simple man who looked deeply into what it means to know God and have a relationship with Jesus.

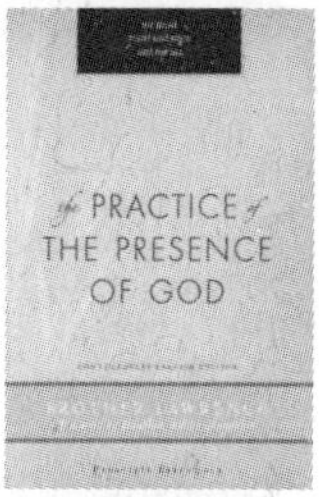

The Practice of the Presence of God

978-1-55725-694-2 | Trade paper, $14.99

In this classic work, Br. Lawrence reveals the secrets of daily, moment-by-moment fellowship with God—full of realistic honesty, friendliness, and simplicity.

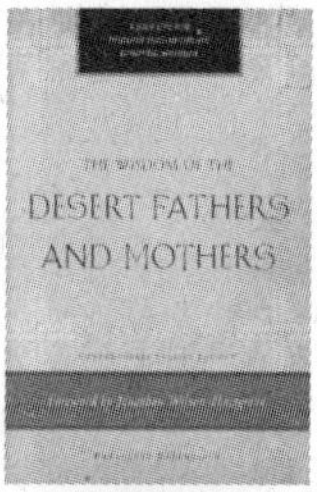

The Wisdom of the Desert Fathers and Mothers

978-1-55725-780-2 | Trade paper, $14.99

This volume contains Athanasius's famous *The Life of St. Antony*, St. Jerome's *The Life of Paul the Hermit*, and the collected sayings of many of the desert fathers and mothers.

Little Talks with God

978-1-55725-779-6 | Trade paper, $15.99

While in an ecstatic trance, St. Catherine of Siena dictated *The Dialogue*. She offers up petitions to God; gives instruction on discernment, obedience and truth; and reveals her famous image of Christ as the Bridge.

Available at bookstores everywhere.

PARACLETE PRESS www.paracletepress.com 1-800-451-5006

You may also be interested in . . .

Three Ways of Loving God

St. Augustine, St. Teresa of Avila,
St. Francis de Sales

978-1-61261-499-1 | Trade paper, $13.99

Praying with Your Whole Heart

St. Augustine, St. Catherine of Siena,
Anonymous, and Thomas à Kempis

978-1-61261-507-3 | Trade paper, $13.99

These thematic collections of spiritual teachings from some of the best Christian writers in history are sure to be popular with book study groups, Centering prayer gatherings, adult Christian formation, and individual spiritual reading.

Available at bookstores everywhere.

PARACLETE PRESS www.paracletepress.com 1-800-451-5006